SOUL FOOD and
Spirit Vittles

Volume One

MARY JANE HOLT

Mary Jane Holt

SOUL FOOD and
Spirit Vittles

Volume One

MARY JANE HOLT

INTRODUCTION

In 1966, just out of high school and working as a nurse's aid at the local hospital, I saw my first suicide victim brought through the emergency room doors. It was called a "self-inflicted gunshot wound to the head." Only hours before, however, he apparently had been a hurting man who decided there was no hope left and no reason to go on living. I suspect he was overwhelmed by the aloneness which engulfed him in the midst of his "hopelessness." In the years since, there have been others whose paths have crossed mine, others who have died at their own hand. On the following pages I share from the corners of my heart, a heart which longs to tell a world of hurting people that it is okay to feel, to grow, and to come to know:

You Are Not Alone and There Is Hope.

I AM
the Bread of Life.
Whoever comes to me will never go hungry and
whoever believes in me with never thirst.

~~~

"If you love me, feed my sheep."
Jesus

Somewhere
beyond today
out on the edge of tomorrow
oblivious
to all our yesterdays
we shall stand
with but a faint memory
of today's pain
for it, too, shall fade
and only Love shall remain

< >

VICTORIOUS

It had been a long day.

Discouragement knocked
but an exhausted Faith
ignored the sound
so Discouragement knocked again
while Faith continued to ignore him
throughout the almost endless evening
yet Discouragement continued to knock
again and again
and Doubt came to stand by his side.

Tired and troubled
Faith turned to Hope
who silently appeared
somehow from somewhere
"should we confront them?"
she whispered
as Discouragement and Doubt
continued to knock
louder and louder.

Faith and Hope
together turned
- not to open the door -
but to their Father in prayer
and
the long day and long night
saw the morning dawn
to find Peace
make his presence known
and the knocking grew quieter.

With the fullness of the new day
came once more
a new knock upon the door
this time
Faith opened it to find
Charity
battle-worn and weary
alone on the porch
victorious
and now abideth
Faith, Hope and Charity
all through the long days and nights of our lives
for Charity never fails and Peace forever reigns.
< >

ECCLESIASTES 3:10-13

I have seen the travail, which God hath given to the sons of men to be exercised in it. He hath made every thing beautiful in his time: also he hath set the world in their heart, so that no man can find out the work that God maketh from the beginning to the end. I know that there is no good in them, but for a man to rejoice, and to do good in his life. And also that every man should eat and drink, and enjoy the good of all his labour, it is the gift of God.

Throwing Caution to the Wind

Throwing all caution to the wind
I let my words fall where they may.
I let my heart write what it would say
to people everywhere
who long to know they are not alone.

Even when loved ones are suddenly gone,
hopes crushed and dreams shattered,
though all that ever mattered
lies broken at their feet,
I hope my words will fall there, too,
Like rose petals of promise
whose fragrance wafts upward
into the recesses of the soul
which would refuse to face another day
if it were not for these words
my heart so longs to say,

God's grace is sufficient,
His love everlasting,
His way not always our way,
is what I would say
to that one who fears to face tomorrow.
Were God's judgments not tempered
with unending mercy,
none could withstand
the touch of His hand.
but His hand reaches down,
not to hurt or destroy;
instead,
His hand reaches out to you and to me
to guide us gently
when there's not enough light to see
the path which lies before us,
or glimpse the goal that's just ahead,
when there is not enough faith to envision
a victory on some distant shore,
when there is only anger and anguish and pain,
when it seems there is no way to win
and nothing to gain
by continuing to trudge along in this world.

Then, that hand, His hand,
reaches out to touch His own,
and with a gentle nudge that's His alone,
He turns His children toward the Morning Light,
with a firm assurance once again
that the darkness they have known for so long
will know its appointed end.
Indeed,
I must throw all caution to the wind
and let my pen fall where it may,
for in the end,
I, too, find hope
in what my heart does long to say.

< >

JEREMIAH 29:11-13

For I know the thoughts that I think toward you, saith the Lord, thoughts of peace, and not of evil, to give you an expected end. Then shall ye call upon me, and ye shall go and pray unto me, and I will hearken unto you. And ye shall seek me, and find Me, when ye shall search for me with all your heart.

There is a Need

In many a life there is a heart
that has been broken one too many times
and it shrivels
as it withdraws more and more from folks
singing no songs,
hearing not hope's soft, inviting chimes.

In many a heart there is a soul
whose dreams are dying,
fading fast away
with visions of all eternity now growing dim
and hope near gone for the dawn of day.

In many a soul there is a hunger
that's strong enough to overrule the heart.
It's a hunger
to know One Who can ease the pain
a hunger He put there from the start.

< >

LUKE 7:50

He (Jesus) said to the woman,
Thy faith hath saved thee; go in peace.

God?
Yes?
Where are you?
I am here.
I cannot see you.
I see you.
I cannot feel your presence.
I am near.
I am frustrated, angry and afraid.
I can tell.
I am worried.
I am not.
I have so much I must do!
I am watching.
I am tired.
I offer rest.
I cannot accept, just now.
I know...
I do not understand.
I do.
What can I say? What can I do?
I? Must it always be "I"?
I mean we, what must we do?
Anything. Everything. All things.
What ever really needs doing.
                    My child?
                         Yes?
                    I am here.
                         I know.   < >

The Way I Take

Lord, You know the way I take.
Even before the road ahead
Comes into my view,
Before one word is ever said,
I know
It's known by You.

Lord, You know all my struggles,
The things of earth that tempt me so.
You know my faith is weak;
That obedience comes so slow.
and yet,
Such peace You speak.

< >

One Day

God, there is one part of my heart
where pain still seems to be hiding.
I have felt set apart right from the start,
and, so often,
I feel like crying.
I cannot make the hurt go away.
Is it here to stay?
Will it always be this way?
How I wish life could be easier!

Child, look to Me and understand,
It is best to leave some things alone.
Hold tight to My hand, as you walk the land;
Someday you will know as you are known.
For now, there must be darkness and light.

Stand
Learn to fight;
You will make it through this long night,
And, one day, life will be easier.
< >

II CORINTHIANS 4:16-18

For which cause we faint not; but though our outward man perish, yet the inward man is renewed day by day. For our light affliction, which is but for a moment, worketh for us a far more exceeding and eternal weight of glory; While we look not at the things which are seen, but at the things which are not seen: for the things which are seen are temporal; but the things which are not seen are eternal.

Enough?

You may ask me if God is enough.
I shall smile as I answer,
"Quite enough," I shall say.
The road may be long and weary
but He stays by our side day after day.
You see, He has traveled to every place.
There is no destination we reach
where He has not been before.
Every temptation that we ever face
He goes through it with us.
He walks first through every door.
He has never turned His back on us.
He holds our hand
through sorrow, pain, and shame.
I admit ... His face we cannot always see
but the great "I AM" is true to His name.
I KNOW
for whenever I pause to look back
coincidences beyond imagination
mark my path and His presence is a fact
far beyond Life's most complex explanations
< >

ISAIAH 1:18

"Come now, and let us reason together..."

Eternity

It is when friends fail,
dreams fade,
or a life-threatening illness strikes,
that the reality of God's presence
and His willingness to be involved
in every detail of our lives becomes apparent.
That reality
gets one through the dark nights
filled with loneliness, fear, confusion,
anger and pain
until the morning comes.
Then in the light of His presence
all other realities grow dim
and lose their control
as an awareness of the eternal takes hold.
For indeed,
what does it all matter in the light of eternity?

< >

ROMANS 8:28

And we know that all things work together for good to them that love God, to them who are the called according to His purpose.

Doubts?

We are special, you and I,
made in the image of God.
He our Creator, desires to communicate with us,
to reason with us.
just as we desire to reason with our own children.
Question God?
Yes, I have.
It seems to me He welcomes my questions,
knowing only as I ask will I learn and grow.
Wonder why He works as He does
in the affairs of men?
Yes, I do; and sometimes, I cry
because I cannot understand His ways.
But doubt His existence?
No more, for I have seen Him in butterflies,
sunsets and children.
And I have seen His faithfulness
toward the living and the dying.
Questions?
The questions remain – for Him and about him.
But, doubts?
The doubts are gone.

< >

REVELATION 21:6

And he said unto me,
It is done. I am Alpha and Omega, the beginning and
the end. I will give unto him that is athirst of the
fountain of the water of life freely.

At His Fountain

If we drink from His well,
we can speak,
we can stand,
we can walk,
we can fly,
in His power
down the paths which lay before us,
into the valleys,
onto the mountaintops,
thru desert places,

For from His fountain
which never runs dry
flows water that sustains.
When other sources of nourishment,
however psychologically nourishing
they may be,
dry up with famine or neglect,
rot with age or contamination,
or just change directions with the times,
the cool clear water of His well flows on
to quench our thirst,
to cool our brow...

We ask why.
We ask how.
And He answers softly,
as we rest
in the shade
of His shadow.
He holds out His cup
longing for us
to sip from it.

And He says,
My thoughts are not your thoughts, My child,
neither are your ways My ways,
but you must walk on,
for I am near.
As the heavens are higher than the earth,
so are My ways higher than your ways,
and My thoughts higher than your thoughts,
but My spirit longs
to be One with yours.
I long to lead you into riches
of which this world knows nothing,
a wealth incomprehensible to those
who choose not to trust Me.

I offer
Love
Joy
Peace
Patience
Kindness
Goodness
Faithfulness
Gentleness
and Self-control.
I offer rest unto your soul,
and I offer Myself to have and to hold.
I long for you to know Me,
to know Me completely,
to be One with Me,
How I long for it, My child,
for you to know Me and to love Me,
as I know and love you!
Rest here at My well for a time.
Drink from My fountain.
Then trust Me.
Follow Me.
And it shall be
we shall become One.

< >

I CORINTHIANS 4:4-5

For I know nothing by myself; yet am I not hereby justified: but he that judgeth me is the Lord. Therefore judge nothing before the time, until the Lord come, who both will bring to light the hidden things of darkness, and will make manifest the counsels of the hearts: and then shall every man have praise of God.

Exposure

There are corners of our hearts
where pain hides,
pain which emanates
from a few almost forgotten memories,
memories hidden well beneath life's surface.
Then, one day,
Courage comes walking
into the present moment
with an offer to lead the way into the past.
He carries a strange Light,
designed to expose
the hidden thoughts of the heart.

Courage knows exposure will bring Victory.
Victory will be accompanied by Freedom,
and only those willing to risk the journey
will come to know Freedom well.
As the Light of Courage shines into our hearts
it slowly penetrates every area
where old emotional debris
has been harbored over the years.

In His wisdom,
God allows circumstances to come our way
which sometimes cause us to recoil.

Suppression
is a mechanism which is frequently used
when life becomes a bit too painful.
And, yes,
I suppose we can take to the grave
a whole lifetime of suppressed memories...
But, what a waste.
To have had life take so much from us
it seems only fair
that something be given back.

I believe God works in myriad ways
and sometimes it is on the journey backward
or inward
where He is found in all His sufficiency.

Occasionally,
it is in seeking to know ourselves
that we come to know Him.
We are His creation,
made in His image,
and He has a vested interest in us.

In sincerely desiring
with all our hearts,
to know Him
and in never giving up the quest,
Victory comes,
Truth is revealed,
and Freedom for all eternity becomes ours.
Sometimes, it is a fragrance,
or a sunset,
or the feel of a brisk and refreshing wind
on a scorching summer day
which triggers the rebirth of that first memory.
As it surfaces,
fear may knock,
wanting to come in for one last visit.
Do not give entrance.
Let Courage lead
and let His light shine.
The penetrating beams
will enable you to see how to clean house.
Joy will knock shortly,
Laughter lies just around the bend.
Make way.
Prepare for their visit.
Perhaps they will stay this time.

< >

Perspective

At first my prayer was
"God, hurry please and get me well
I have so much to do;"
and then my prayer became,
"God, thank you for this special time
I have to spend with you."

time to recognize anew
the value of health and strength
but to grasp also
the courage it takes to learn to lean

time to listen and hear once more
the song of the distant mockingbird
to witness the red birds, blue birds and robins
as they adorn the front yard
to watch the squirrels romp and play out back
while a whole covey of quail
feeds in the turnip patch

time to appreciate the beauty,
joy and peace of aloneness

time to read books, magazines and articles
acquired in recent months
when it seemed there was no time to read them

time to renew ageless friendships
with old and familiar books
and explore again
the well worn pages of my favorite

time to listen to good music
and the heart thoughts of a friend

time to care and share
and know anew the value of prayer

At first my prayer was
"God, hurry please and get me well
I have so much to do;"
and then my prayer became,
"God, thank you for this special time
I have to spend with you."
< >

PROVERBS 18:24

A man that hath friends must shew himself friendly: and there is a friend that sticketh closer than a brother.

Regrets

Regrets?
I don't think there are any;
I once thought there might be many.

It's a strange world we live in
with a heartache now and again.
but God's hand has a way
of working with me
as the Potter works with the clay
and then I can see
that what brought us so much pain
was ordained for mine and your gain.

Regrets?
I once thought there might be many;
Now, I don't think there are any.

< >

To Friends Who Fail

I can trust no one
cried a wounded soul
for all that's been done
was wrong and cruel.

Then the Voice called to him!

As he looked above through faith grown dim
it was Christ alone he saw standing there.

All others gone.

Did he dare to share the cares, the pain
with this lone One ?

Inching nearer to this One who had come
his heart could see clearer
where He had come from
and the darkness which
had long clouded his way
and shattered his dreams
now turned to day
in the presence of this One, God's Son
Who knew all he'd ever done.

Yes, there stood Jesus
with arms open wide
calling him by name
bidding him come hide
in the shadow of His grace and love
a place of security
where he could abide for a time

And as he drew near
he could hear Him softly whisper
of a promised end
to all the aloneness he'd known
for so many years.
"I will walk with you," He said,
"over these next long miles
and I will not fail you.
Do not harbor hatred.
Don't be bitter or mean.
For if they had come through for you,
you would never have seen my love for you,
and you would never have known
how long I have waited
to come to you, to hold you
to be there for you.
It was so long I have had to wait
and I had waited long enough."

< >

Betrayal

He wanted to smile
as his mind began to wander back
down through the lonely years.
Recalling little laughter
knowing anew the tears
he had cried alone
on that desert journey
where no one had known
the emptiness.
There had been no one
with whom to share
the brokenness of a heart
where the bitter anguish of betrayal
had reigned for a season.
Loved ones lost for a time.

He wondered at the ways God chooses
to work in the affairs of men.
False accusations were so unfair
and always it seemed
there were so few who cared.
Yet, freedom had come, and honor,
and now – this moment!
He gave them the grain.

Their very lives lay in the palm of his hand
and as the light of understanding dawned
suddenly he could see
beyond the pain of yesterday
beyond all faults and failures, including his own
beyond the grief
his father must have known
beyond the terror
their hungry hearts must know today.
Alas! He wondered as he glimpsed
the plan for all the age!

– Eternal Truth –

He saw it! He had known he would.
"You, you meant evil against me,"
he said, "but God ... God meant it for good."
And he smiled.
< >

GENESIS 50:20

But as for you, ye thought evil against me;
but God meant it unto good, to bring to pass,
as it is this day, to save much people alive.

Alone in the Storm

I have felt alone in the storm.
I have known the paralysis of fear
and in its grip heard the reassuring voice
of the fearless One whisper softly,
"Lo, I am with you always."
I have known the fury of defeat
and in such knowledge,
heard the voice of victory
call calmly to me
from the next room,
"Lo, I am with you always."
I have known fierce crippling pain
and in the midst,
heard indescribable compassion
in the voice of One
whose understanding made it bearable,
"Lo, I am with you always."
I have known bleak despair
and in its hold
heard One whose Father once turned away
speak gently to remind me
of His continuing presence,
"Lo, I am with you always."

I have known a cold darkness
and in the black mist
heard the voice of the Light of the world
burst forth with a promise
of gladness and guidance
"Lo, I am with you always."
I have known anger and its prison
heard the tender voice of One
Who knows me so well
Who understands my thoughts from afar
Who knows my downsitting and my uprising
Who is intimately acquainted with all my ways
Who sees my going out and my coming in
Who scrutinizes my path and my lying down
Whose presence is too wonderful to proclaim
Whose existence cannot be explained
One Who eases in and out
of the avenues of my life
as the wind that blows,
permitting me to know not
from whence it comes or where it goes.
I only know that it moves my hair
and cools my cheek and continually whispers
ever so softly and tenderly,
"Lo, I have been, I am, and I will be with you
always, even unto the end of the world!"
I have felt alone in the storm, but I never was!

< >

PSALM 3:3-5

But thou, O Lord, art a shield for me; my glory, and the lifter up of mine head. I cried unto the Lord with my voice, and he heard me out of his holy hill. Selah. I laid me down and slept; I awaked; for the Lord sustained me.

The Organ Donor

somebody died somewhere last year
and
somebody cried

today
another, in wonder
sheds a tear
for her whose eye sees
another's child at play
and thrills to call him her child, too
for her whose heart
throbs with a borrowed passion
for the one she loves, but never knew
for her whose skin
feels the cool damp magic
of a shared Sunday morning dew

somebody lives to laugh today
somebody gives her all joyfully
for her who gave her all away
< >

PSALM 91:1

He that dwelleth in the secret place of the most High shall abide under the shadow of the Almighty.

Vulnerability's Toll

You say you have tried,
that you have done all you can,
that vulnerability takes too great a toll,
yet, I ask you once more to climb over that wall.
The barrier that went up such a long time ago
seems insurmountable to you now.
I know.
You think there is no way you can bear
to let your feelings show
one more time.
You say
nobody really wants to be there
when you need them to be,
to know your struggle,
to feel your pain
to share your hurt.
But try one more time
just one quick leap!
Risk it and let Him be
the friend He wants
so much to be
then you will see
that though you will assuredly hurt again,
you will never hurt alone again.
< >

A true poet once told me that a true poet never has a message to share, only words - magical words, musical words, wondrous words. It is a poet's fascination with words and language that leads him to play with words, to commune with them and to allow them to commune with him. The "poem" on the next page is a throwing together of words. Following that page I will tell you why I threw them together because I profess not to be a true poet.

Words intrigue me only as one of the manifold avenues along which I celebrate life. All of God's creation fascinates me. So, because I cannot personally laugh with, cry with, hug or hold every person with whom my heart does so long to commune, I write. I write with a purpose. I write to tell you that you are not alone in your struggle, your pain, your loss. Nor are you alone in times of triumph, success, victory.

I write to tell you there is Hope.

We are wonderfully and uniquely made. Together, we can master whatever we are required to overcome. It is in accepting the grace to grow, sometimes together, sometimes apart, that we evolve in our shared and continuing celebration of life.

< >

HOPE!

damp lower level windows swing slightly open
never wide enough
to fling forth a faded invitation
to a weakened army on the march
forever counting the cost of clearing away
the dark debris of a hard fought battle
lost
unknown victory
cherished from afar
never realized
since the windows only swing open
wide enough and long enough
for but a fleeting glimpse
of an ever elusive healing
while Hope knocks in vain
at the closed and barred door
of a still sad and staggering soul

NO! NO! NO!
Run to that door! Unlock it!
Open it NOW. Feast on HOPE!
LET LOVE WIN!

< >

As I played with words, through HOPE, on the preceding page, I was talking about how people sometimes grow to be comfortable and prefer the familiarity of grief and pain over healing. They know they hurt, that they are sick, and they may peep out of a tiny soul window every now and then to see if there is any hope on some distant horizon, but for various reasons, i.e. guilt, attachment, cowardice, laziness, etc. they refuse to courageously, even eagerly, walk over to the door of their soul, swing it wide and let hope come in.

Please play with your own words here:

_____

_____

_____

_____

_____

_____

_____

_____

_____

_____

_____

_____

_____

< >

"Here's what you could have done if you had been willing to forgive and let go of all the hurt, regret and bitterness. The spirit that conquers is able to forget in order to forge ahead in God's love." It was 1986 and Dr. Charles Stanley's insightful words came over the radio airwaves to settle forever into the deepest recesses of my heart. I was on my way to work at the time, so I pulled off the road and jotted down his pearls of wisdom on the back of a page I tore from a prescription pad I had in my lab coat pocket. I never rewrote them, or typed them up all neat and pretty. They still rest on that piece of paper where I hastily recorded them that morning. They rest there, and in my heart.

<>

On Conquering...

Again: "Here's what you could have done if you had been willing to forgive and let go of all the hurt, regret and bitterness..."

How much wasted energy do we expend nurturing old hurts, clinging to yesterday's regrets, and claiming all the bitterness that our past says we have every right to feel?
How many times do we recall, with pain or anger or frustration, some memory from days, months, or years past, some recollection which surfaces to color the present a drab shade of gray and rob us of the invaluable joy and energy which should be ours in this present moment?
The spirit that conquers is indeed able to forget in order to forge ahead in God's love.
There are a number of approaches one might use to better cope with the memory of a painful past, and overcome the negative ways it influences the present.

One approach might be to mentally and emotionally travel back into yesterday, and recall events and feelings which greatly influence today's actions. Circumstances or happenings from the past may be evaluated in an effort to determine to what extent they have shaped, or are shaping, the present. Sometimes, the understanding which such an inward journey produces brings healing which is almost instantly followed by lifestyle changes. At other times, needed change comes slowly. Though such inner travel occasionally can make for a long and painful journey, it can be a journey which may prove to be well worth the effort.

Another approach is to simply recognize behavior which is counterproductive or destructive in one's life, then determine what is the appropriate behavior in order to achieve desired goals and go from there – that is, just recognize "wrong" or inappropriate behavior, acknowledging at the same time what is "right" or appropriate behavior, and then change one's behavior patterns. I am told it can be that simple for some people.

Perhaps, however, a combination of the two approaches can be more effective. Why? Because it makes sense to do some reminiscing along with self-evaluation, when we try to define the negative, unproductive, energy wasting behavior which shapes the present day. Such definition gives direction as we journey backwards in an attempt to uncover the hurts and regrets and bitterness from yesterday which so strongly influence us now.

It is in our power to face the challenges which come with the dawning of each new day with love in our hearts for others, hope for the future, and the courage to let go of the past; or we can confront each sunrise with the same old hurts, regrets and bitterness which shaped so many yesteryears. In-depth professional therapy is not always necessary to help us act appropriately. Sometimes, life just requires that we forgive and forget in order to forge ahead in God's love.

< >

I SAMUEL 3:15

And Samuel lay until the morning, and opened the doors of the house of the Lord. And Samuel feared to shew Eli the vision.

Three Visions

It was September, 1986. On Labor Day weekend I was at the city auditorium in Thomasville, Georgia for the annual All Night Gospel Singing. There, I had the first of three visions that prompted me to take the road which has led to where I am today.

Visions were only something I had read about in the Bible until that night. As a matter of fact I didn't believe in visions until then. I'd had my share of dreams while I was sleeping, dreams that later came true. That was weird enough, but I had grown used to them. Visions were something else! I don't know what having a vision means to others. I couldn't begin to intelligently discuss the subject. Then that's the trouble with so many things we can't explain. It is too easy to dismiss what we can't understand with our ever-so-limited intellect. There was no dismissing my first vision.

In the midst of the music and a tremendous air of celebration, with my sister sitting to my right and strangers all around, suddenly I saw a miniature wagon train on the stage, circling The Galileans, a talented singing group from Texas. Just like in an old western movie. And the wagon train was being called to a halt, making a circle for the evening. It was a split second kind of never to be forgotten eternal thing. I do not know how the experience manifested itself on my countenance, but my sister asked what was wrong. It was so vivid for me that I asked if she had seen it too.

Not hardly.

She watched me rather closely for the rest of the evening. I decided then that my wagon train was not something I ought to tell folks about right away. If she had trouble believing, what would the rest of the world think?

The following Sunday night, after the evening worship service, I went to the altar of my home church to discuss with God the strange occurrence I could not shake off.

While kneeling there pouring out my heart, asking what it meant, if anything, wondering if I had a brain tumor or worse, I had my second vision! This time my eyes were closed in serious silent prayer, but it was just as vivid! It does not remain so clear today as the first and third, but as I recall, in it the wagon master told everybody to prepare to rest for a few days, not just overnight.

It prompted much soul searching on my part for several days.

The next Sunday evening I returned to that same spot at the altar. This time I purposefully went for session three.

I believed.

I knew it would come.

It came.

It was disturbing.

It changed my life.

I saw again the wagon train. In vision number three the person I had perceived to be the wagon master told everybody to hitch up their teams and prepare to move out - everybody but me. He told me to unload everything from my wagon and set my animals free.

I protested, "But how will I cross the mountains?"

"Take my hand and I will lead you, we are going to walk together across the mountains."

For two years prior to this series of visions, I had felt "called" (another word I had a hard time with until it happened to me) to pursue the activities and professions I now enjoy so much. Perhaps haunted or mysteriously led would apply here as well. On Monday morning, following the third vision, I turned in my resignation at the family practice office where I had worked for six years. It was not easy to leave a staff and patients who were like family, but I had mountains to climb and a Personal Guide was waiting.

The best was yet to come.

< >

Once more...

I SAMUEL 3:15

And Samuel lay until the morning, and opened the doors of the house of the Lord. And Samuel feared to shew Eli the vision.

I know how Samuel felt. For many years I told no one about my three visions. There have been other dreams and visions since then, and before them, actually. And always there have been the dreams. I no longer fear. "Speak Lord, I am listening" comes easier now. - mjh

Work To Be Done

Early one Sunday morning in late January, 1988, unable to sleep, I slipped out of bed in the predawn hours, reached for my Bible and settled in at the dining room table for a spell. There was much unrest in my soul, a growing unsettledness I could not understand. Tears flowed as I searched the Scriptures and prayed. I wondered about the unexplained sense of urgency that consumed me.

I did not know until two weeks later that my father, engulfed in his own struggles, had also awakened early during those predawn hours. As I sat at my table, he sat at his desk across the miles, reviewing the notes for the sermon he would deliver later that morning. He must have known it would be his last.

Two souls, unable to sleep, in search of a way to express that which stirred within their hearts - my father preparing his last sermon, "It Is Finished" and I, penning my upcoming newspaper column, "Work To Be Done."

There never seems to be enough time to do all that needs to be done. I express an occasional desire to slow down, to talk with God and faithful old friends more often. I long for the luxury of laughing and crying together about so many experiences we have shared. Such thoughts inevitably lead me to hope Heaven will permit such luxury.

Indeed, Heaven may grant us that option but for now there is work to do. Someday, maybe we all can slow down a bit and reminisce together, in wonder, as we renew old acquaintances in the presence of God. For now there are hungry, hurting and horribly lonely people around the world, even at our own back door. Yes, it is time we were about our Father's business ... for truly there remains a great deal of work to be done.

< >

Many times the story has been told of the old farmer who watched a butterfly struggle for hours to free itself from its cocoon. When he no longer could stand seeing the tiny creature suffer and struggle so intently, he took out his knife and clipped the wrappings which held the butterfly captive. Immediately the beautiful butterfly fell to the ground. Without the strength gained from the struggle the lovely creature could not be prepared to face the challenges which lay ahead. The harsh and apparently painful struggle was nature's way of preparing the butterfly for flight, freedom and life.

< >

"Honey, I know it's hard for you to comprehend, but this time next year you will have a whole different set of problems."

When I met her, it had been a year since she first heard those words. Her world had fallen apart. Her husband had betrayed her. While she was carrying their firstborn he had fathered another woman's child. As the truth surfaced it was almost too harsh and painful to face. She had looked forward for months to the birth of their daughter, and to the three of them sharing their lives together. Now, the routine demands of caring for her baby were her only real diversion; yet, at the same time, the duties of motherhood were a steady reminder of the man who had broken her heart, and destroyed her world. Tears flowed daily.

Crying brought release, though minimal, from the pain, hurt, and hostility which raged within her. Friends and family tried to help. So many loved ones seemed to be there for her, offering encouragement and support. Yet, it never occurred to her that others had suffered as she was suffering.

That other men or women had faced what she'd had to face and survived was a foreign thought. It was beyond her emotional capacity to realize that they not only survived, but continued on with their lives to sometimes find more happiness than they had ever known before. It seemed there would never be any freedom from the nightmare which she relived every day.
Until....
Until the day her dad gently said to her, "Honey I know it's hard for you to comprehend, but this time next year you are going to have a whole different set of problems." And he left it at that. He left her to think her own thoughts, to ponder what he had said. They were the most sobering thoughts she had entertained in months. His words had pierced through the wall of anger and self-pity which had been going up for so many long weeks. His statement, or forecast for the future, made sense. In a strange way, the promise that more problems lay ahead offered hope. Suddenly she knew that all she was experiencing during her present hour of trial would only make her stronger, and more capable of coping with whatever lay ahead.

There would be a future indeed! There would be a tomorrow when things would be different. Maybe her life would be better. Maybe she would be happier. Maybe she would be able to forget some things and forgive those which she could not forget. Assuredly, circumstances would be different! Such thoughts were enough for the moment. Her dad's wisdom and timing would not be appreciated in all their fullness until years later.

Timing, I suppose, is everything.

In time, hope comes.

< >

To hope means to long for something with the expectation of obtainment or fulfillment, of having dreams come to pass.

To hope for a better tomorrow may be all we need in order to gain the needed perspective which will help us overcome present obstacles.

To hope for a better tomorrow does not prevent us from living each today to the fullest.

To hope for that tomorrow might even better equip us to live each and every day more completely, accepting from every moment in time all the wealth and wisdom which might be offered to us.

Though we have no assurance of a tomorrow, the reminder that there probably will be one can sometimes have a most sobering effect.

< >

A Child Leads

She walked into the bathroom where her aunt stood before the long mirror going through the motions women go through prior to applying make-up. The eight-year-old pulled open a drawer and took out her own little stash of mom approved cleanser, toner and moisturizer, products her mother assured her were perfect for the delicate skin of one so young.

Step by step, the two went through their beauty rituals. It was a fun time as the morning sun found its way into every little crevice of the room. Light chatter reigned until the older one started to apply mascara. At that point, the child said, "My mother doesn't let me wear mascara."

"Darling, you don't need it. Your eyelashes are a half inch long. They are dark and beautiful," her aunt said.

"Then, why don't I have a boyfriend?" came the response.

The hand applying the mascara stopped in midair.

A fleeting look of serious desperation fluttered across the face of the little girl in the mirror. Her reflection told her aunt that any reply must not be too light and frivolous.

"Sweetheart, you don't need a boyfriend either. You just need friends, girls and boys. You are much too young to have just one boyfriend. For the next few years, you should be friends with all the boys in your school and at church. Just the way you are friends with the girls."

"But I don't have a lot of friends. I'm shy."

"Well, Darling, the way to have friends is to be friendly. You have to show an interest in others. You don't have to talk about yourself. In fact, you don't have to talk a lot at all. You just have to be interested in other people and know how to ask them questions about themselves."

"What kind of questions?"

"When you go to school tomorrow, pick someone you would like to have for a friend and ask him or her what he or she did over the weekend. Listen closely to their answer then ask another question about their response. Get them to talk about themselves and what they like to do. It's easy."

"Really?"

"Sure, we all want others to show an interest in us and most everybody likes to talk about what they like to do. You will learn a lot about people by asking questions."

The reflection in the mirror had changed. Bright eyes now danced as her little mind considered the advice she was being given. "What do you like to do?" asked her aunt.

"Oh, you know I like to read! And I like to draw. I'm going to take art lessons. I think I might be an artist. (At six, she was going to be a writer. At seven, a physical therapist. And now an artist. What aspirations would come with her ninth year?) And I love to play my piano..."

The aunt hoped that the enthusiastic conversation which ensued would be enough of an example to drive home the truth of her advice. It had been nearly four decades since the age-old instructions had been given to her. It had worked the first time she ever used it and it still worked.

Certainly, to have friends one must be friendly. That's what the wise Sunday School teacher had said. At the same time, she had told her about the "Friend who would stick closer than a brother." Someday soon the aunt would delve a little deeper into the subject of friendship with her niece.

The little one must know about the One Who never moves away or turns away, the One Who will never reject her, the One Whose arms will always welcome her. She must know how to have a conversation with Him. She must talk with the young one about the value of prayer. She must do that soon. She must do it before the roller coaster of adolescence welcomed her aboard. Before life's ups and downs threatened her with too much confusion.

And then the aunt remembered how long it had been since she had asked her Friend about what He had been doing, about how He felt, about His plans, His dreams. It had been too long since they had shared an in-depth conversation. Too long since she had expressed her appreciation for His undying friendship. Too long since she had thanked Him for all the times He had been there for her when others had not.

Indeed, a little child shall lead.

< >

Max Cleland

Oh, how I wanted to turn back at the time, but he inspired me to stay on the road that has brought me to where I am today.
He said, "Sometimes we stand and look back so long and hard at the doors that have closed behind us that we fail to see those opening before us."

Max Cleland's words challenged me to move forward. I am thankful to call him friend.

Once, on a popular television talk show to discuss an upcoming feature a major magazine was going to publish about him, Max was asked why he allowed the photographer to take a nude shot of him going through his morning stretch routine. It was a decision for which he would no doubt come under a degree of criticism. He was no stranger to criticism and he never flinched as he answered his interrogator. My admiration grew.

Then Democratic Senator from Georgia Max had lost an arm and both legs above the knee in Vietnam. His exercise regimen deserved to be recorded. It is good that he agreed to the photos. It is refreshing that he is real. I can't begin to imagine the number of mentally, emotionally or spiritually handicapped (and outwardly whole) individuals who have been inspired by his courage and stamina.

"Life breaks us all," he says as he often quotes Hemingway, "but afterwards we are strong at the broken places."

The strength Max Cleland gained at his broken places has allowed him to aspire to heights to which I suspect no healthy pair of legs could ever have transported him. And the truly extraordinary thing is that with only one arm he has managed to carry many of us with him in his ascent up and over the mountains. To whom does he give credit for his successes? Consistently and without hesitation he tells all it is only by the grace of God and with the help of friends that he is alive and has accomplished anything at all.

And what has he accomplished? He was head of the Veteran's Administration under President Carter. Then he served several terms as Georgia's Secretary of State before aspiring to the Senate seat he held when talking to King. Small feats compared to overcoming the anger, depression, and pain of those early years after the loss of his limbs. Tiny achievements compared to just getting out of bed and getting dressed every morning.

Max is an overcomer and that's what makes him such a vibrant inspiration to all who care to get to know him. That and the fact that he is real. Which brings us to why I suspect he agreed to the feature article in that magazine.

Handicaps are very real. We all have them. Some are visible. Some are not. None are an excuse for failure or a reason for success.

Who we are and what we become is so much more than any one attribute. Regardless of what we may look like on the outside we are whole people on the inside, or we can be.

More often than most of us care to admit, it all boils down to choice. The sum of all that we ever have been makes us what we are today and influences what we will be tomorrow, but always there are choices to be made.

No blog or column and no article, not even a biographical book or documentary can capture the complete and total essence of a person. But sometimes we need glimpses into the lives of those extraordinary individuals who keep climbing against all odds, especially those who reach summit after summit pausing only long enough at the top of each mountain to turn around, reach back, and extend a hand to a fellow traveler.

Life asks many things of us, but the most important request it makes is that we live it, truly live it. Perhaps, in the end, or in eternity, that may be the one thing for which we cannot forgive ourselves. To have been given life and not to have really lived it may be a hard reality to take with one to the grave or beyond.

So to Max Cleland and others like him, I say thank you for your example, your courage, your determination to fully live all the days of your life. Sometimes, I'm not sure God asks any more or less in the end. By the way, Max was asked by a viewer who called the Larry King show that night how he felt about death after he had come so close to dying. He responded, "Death is easy. It's living that's hard."

Why do I often put a spotlight on Max Cleland? No I'm not a Democrat; nor am I a Republican, (surely you have figured out by now that I am an Independent), but I keep a photo of Max in my office and every time I look at it I say, "If he can get up and boldly face the day, I can, too."

< >

Pain, Pain and still more Pain...

I bet your faith's been shaken a time or two by pain. I know the psalmist once wrote that it had been good for him to have been afflicted. In Psalm 119 we find these words, "Thou hast dealt well with Thy servant, O Lord, according unto Thy word. Teach me good judgment and knowledge: for I have believed Thy commandments. Before I was afflicted I went astray: but now have I kept Thy word. Thou art good and doest good; teach me Thy statutes..." And he continues, "It is good for me that I have been afflicted; that I might learn Thy statutes. The law of Thy mouth is better to me than thousands of gold and silver."
I have a problem believing, even thinking that God doles out pain and suffering to teach us the great and small lessons of life. I mean I really have a major struggle with that. I can grasp the idea that we do much to bring a great deal of misery upon ourselves. Not only do we make poor or unwise individual choices from time to time which result in bad habits, illness, or injury, but we live and move in a world which is an ever evolving product of many collective bad choices over the centuries.

Pollution and great waste of our natural resources have taken, and continue to take, their toll. Certainly, no one generation can take all the credit although we today have made some distinct headway in our efforts to foul up things. Maybe it's not too late to turn around though. I feel like much of the environmental chaos we have created for ourselves is almost a direct result of a lazy self-centeredness which so often surfaces, and sometimes rules, in our lives. Always, we seek easier and better ways to accomplish tasks and function in the world today. Yet I have major issues with the "no pain, no gain" concept.

It might have its place in some physical fitness training circles or rehabilitation settings, but sometimes the idea can be taken to an extreme. It's almost like we are promised a reward for enduring pain well.

Rewards for pain? Some things can just be carried too far. Certainly there are events or circumstances, illness or injury which can occur and prompt timely reflection.

As a matter of fact, I have said before, and I shall readily repeat, that even depression can be good when it doesn't come to stay.

Just about anything which causes us to slow down from time to time and take stock of the courses we have chosen, and the tracks we are leaving behind, cannot be all bad.

But think about a society where litigation has become central to the game of life.

For so much of the illness and injury which comes our way we look for someone or something to blame and immediately we get in line to take all our misery and loss into the courtroom.

However, nothing is ever as immediate as we need it to be.

A law suit takes time and the pain must not get better until the law suit is settled.

Right?

I mean, how would it look to a jury being asked to award the victim a few hundred thousand dollars for his or her great pain and suffering if that victim took the stand with a healthy glow?

Hollywood, the news media, our legal system and a deep-seated appreciation for money has taught us better, right?

Along with the psalmist, perhaps we all do have the opportunity to gain much from our afflictions.

The question is,
"What are we out to gain?"

< >

My Awful Wedding Day

Sometimes it feels like only yesterday that I
endured one of the worst days of my life.
The day I married was not a good one.
It was at least 100 degrees and that might have
been in the shade.
I had a headache that defies description to this
day.
I was three months pregnant and had absolutely
no assurance that I was doing the right thing.
That was before I said "I do." As we drove north
and the sun sank in the west it grew cooler.
My headache got better.
The pregnancy? That stayed with me for
another six months.
And the idea of commitment that had been
absent prior to the vows began to set in.
On that drive northward I prayed for wisdom
and peace and the courage to stand by my
commitment to my husband.
God hears and answers sincere prayers.
The average person felt we were one of those
couples doomed to become a divorce statistic.
Everything was stacked against us, they said.
And it was.

We had not known one another long enough. We were starting our life together as three instead of two. They said we wouldn't make it. The next time you are inclined to listened to what "they" may be saying, please know they are often wrong.

In fact, just like there are times when it seems like only yesterday that we started our journey together, there also are times when it seems like we have been together forever.

Some contradiction, huh?

How have we pulled it off?

We have done it only by being willing to take commitment seriously and truly by the grace of God, and not necessarily in that order.

Marriage is not easy. Nothing worthwhile is. There is no denying that it all began with sex, really good sex. The physical attraction was the motivating factor and we did not take time to know one another. But, once the "I dos" were said we resolved to do just that - get to know one another, that is.

At this writing, many decades later, we are still working on the project. For the most part it's been fun.

At times it was for the children that I remained committed. Then there were those moments when I just hung in there while I tried to decide who I was. Yes, the search continues well past puberty. So, even if you don't do it all in the order it probably should be done, marriage can still work.

Would I count my marriage a success? Absolutely.

I don't quite know when it happened, but my husband eventually became my dearest friend. We now have a strong history together and we are proud of it. But more than anything we are thankful for it.

On our honeymoon we stopped by a nursing home in North Georgia where his sister worked. She introduced us as newlyweds to a resident there. The little old lady beckoned us close to her and admonished us to never let the sun go down on our wrath. "Don't ever go to sleep angry," she said.

I cannot begin to tell you how many times over the years I wanted to go back and shake that dear little old lady and make her take back her admonition. Why? Because Daniel took her advice as the gospel I now suppose it was.

Any normal, healthy woman will tell you in a split second, however, that a good burst of anger cannot and should not be turned off just because the sun is going down. Not hardly. We much prefer to nurture our anger, to let it smolder and become all it should be. My husband, however, has never allowed me that luxury.

Granted, we have had more than one sleepless night. But we have seldom gone to sleep angry. The only time I have ever been able to hold on to a good spell of anger was if I somehow managed not to let him know how mad I was. Now tell me how much fun that could be.
It's odd though.
Today as I write this I cannot recall the last time I was angry with the man. It's strange how getting to know someone, understanding them, and being their friend can cast such a different light on everything.

< >

Coping with Stress

We must never lose perspective. Ever tried to paint a landscape without proper perspective? Things lose their rightful place in the setting. So it is in life. Without a proper perspective, things lose their rightful place in the day to day routines of our lives.

So, how do we maintain a rightful perspective? First, we have to relax a bit.

My dad used to laugh. When he had about reached his limit, he would laugh. It was the same as crying for many females I have known, self included. Both the laughter and the crying bring relief of sorts. I always envied Daddy's laughter. It seemed to relax him and give him a renewed energy.

Those of us who choose to cry are left with red noses, tense and swollen faces, and a bit of fatigue. Oh, don't get me wrong, crying has its place. In some situations, there is nothing better. Depending on the circumstances, a good cry or a good laugh, work their own miracles for the body and soul.

Second, we must bring our breathing under control. Check it out the next time you get really bent out of shape over something trivial, or even earthshaking. Really pay attention to your breathing patterns. Chances are a few good, deep breaths (very deep), taken in and breathed out slowly (very slowly) will do wonders. The simple act of choosing to check out your breathing patterns gives you a break from the stress of the moment. You make a choice and act on that choice and it releases you from the grip in which the emotion of the moment holds you.

Third, you ask for help. Some folks might choose to follow some respected chain of command. Me? More often than not I go straight to the top. How on earth or in heaven He pulls it off, I don't know, but God always has time to hear me out. Once I have spoken with Him, then I will check out any other reasonable chain of command that may be in place. I may or may not follow such a chain, depending on the circumstances and how much time I may have to solve the problem at hand.

So, where are we now in our efforts to cope with stress? We have laughed, or cried, taken a deep breath and whispered a prayer.

Ah, the question!

Again:

"What does it all matter in the light of eternity?" I suppose the answer to that question depends on your faith. Your personal religious beliefs will dictate much of your future action in times of great stress. After you have followed steps one, two and three, to some degree your religious or faith convictions will kick in.

Now, I won't pretend to have the wisdom to tell you what to do after that happens. But your heart will respond if you let it. I hope you share my awareness of a great and wonderful God, a heavenly Father who cares deeply about every aspect of our lives. If you do, and if you turn to Him at some point during your time of irritation, pain, loss, or deep grief, then you will more than likely be afforded a strange kind of peace that will get you through anything.

Too often, circumstances
are far beyond our control;
but seldom, if ever
do we lose the right to choose
how we will respond to those circumstances.

It's those tiny, almost inconspicuous threads woven into the minute details of life where I find God most often reveals himself.

And thus my faith continues to grow.

Like one Monday night I lay in bed wondering where I get off speaking so boldly about and for Jesus Christ.

"How do I know?" I asked myself. "What is it about Jesus? What makes Him worthy of the role He has in my life and the lives of so many believers?"

You would think we would reach some plateau where the questions cease.

I keep hoping, but for now the queries keep coming.

After hours of prayerful searching I reached conclusions I have reached many times in the past.

Jesus Christ is worthy because He understands.

He identifies with me.

He has been where I am.

He has faced every temptation I have ever faced.

He feels what I feel.

I recalled again how He prayed in the garden for another way.

As the cross loomed near He wanted an out.
Yes, He was God, but He was human, too.
The one big difference is He wore His humanity
without sin. As an unblemished lamb He died for
me; in my place He gave His life so that I could
have eternal life.

Okay, I know many things must often come into
play before you can recognize Jesus for all He
has been, is, and can be for you. I wish I could
help you there, but I can't. Ultimately you are on
your own in that search (we all are). The best I
can do is tell you a story or two from time to
time. So, I shall continue with what prompted my
Monday night thoughts.

I'd had surgery six weeks earlier. It went well. I
was happy until the end of the third week when
the first hives appeared. For a week they
popped out at random with no rhyme or reason
to where and why they were appearing.

It was no big deal. I am an allergic person and
no stranger to hives. I don't think I even began
to put two and two together until the day I woke
up with my face swollen and I was having
trouble breathing. I live more than thirty minutes
from the hospital, so I immediately took what
medication I had on hand.

Before we reached the hospital I was breathing better, but starting to react to the drug I had taken to help me breathe. I spent the better part of the day at the medical facility. By the time I left for home, yet another drug or two had been added to the arsenal I detested taking every day. An attitude was setting in.

On Monday evening the depression grabbed hold and held tight for about four to six hours. On Tuesday morning as I prepared to go to Atlanta to see more doctors, anger became the dominant emotion. My allergist confirmed suspicions that I had begun to react to the sutures which were now being absorbed by my body. Then the new surgeon, with whom I had to consult after seeing the allergist, outlined the various options I had for continued treatment for problems that still were not solved.

With distasteful thoughts bobbing all around in my mind I asked my son (and chauffeur) to take me to the Buckhead Diner for lunch.

He frowned, but drove in that direction.

After a couple of minutes I told him to turn around and head south, that we'd find some place neat for lunch on the southside. He grinned.

As he drove I began to say my thank yous to my heavenly Father for my son and all he had done for me in recent days and weeks.

When I spoke aloud again I said, "Take me to Hooters for lunch."
"What?!"
"Take me to Hooters on 19&41."
"Why?"
"Isn't that your favorite place to eat?"
"It is. They make great chicken sandwiches."
"Then let's have a chicken sandwich."
He drove to Hooters.
We made our way to the only empty table we could see.
It was in the back corner on the left.
Close to the cash register where all the waitresses in their skimpy costumes congregated.
I could see my son was pleased.
The sandwiches were delicious.
The service was excellent.
And, yes, the waitresses were beautiful.

But the sight to behold lay outside the building. After I finished my meal I sat gazing out the window at the rain falling on the pavement. I love the rain.

My gaze ventured beyond the parking lot, past another expanse of pavement and through a patch of woods to a huge white statute of Jesus Christ kneeling in prayer.

I gasped.

"What's wrong?" asked my son.
"It's Jesus, kneeling in prayer."
He walked around the table to see for himself.
"There's a cemetery over there through the woods. You just can't see the rest of it," he said.

He had no way of knowing my thoughts over the past 48 hours. And I could not explain at that moment what the vision meant to me. So I just tell my stories with full knowledge that those inconspicuous threads woven into the minute details of life not only cause my faith to continue to grow, but they bind us all together in strange and unique ways as God works His miracles in and through us when we least expect it.

<>

MATTHEW 25:31-40

When the Son of man shall come in his glory, and all the holy angels with him, then shall he sit upon the throne of his glory: And before him shall be gathered all nations, and he shall separate them one from another, as a shepherd divideth His sheep from the goats: And he shall set the sheep on his right hand, but the goats on the left. Then shall the King say unto them on his right hand, Come, ye blessed of my Father, inherit the kingdom prepared for you from the foundation of the world: For I was an hungred, and ye gave me meat: I was thirsty, and ye gave me drink: I was a stranger, and ye took me in: Naked, and ye clothed me: I was sick, and ye visited me: I was in prison, and ye came unto me. Then shall the righteous answer him, saying, Lord, when saw we thee an hungred, and fed Thee? or thirsty, and gave Thee drink? When saw we thee a stranger, and took Thee in? or naked, and clothed Thee? Or when saw we thee sick, or in prison, and came unto thee? And the King shall answer and say unto them, Verily I say unto you, Inasmuch as ye have done it unto one of the least of these my brethren, ye have done it unto me.

What Happened?

The maximum security inmate was what many would have called a hardened criminal. He had laughed, mocked and even threatened those who had expressed concern for the welfare of his soul over the years. Then, one day, all that changed. He began to study the Book he had made fun of for so long. The Bible became important to him. Over time, what he was learning from the timeless pages of God's Word started to affect his daily living at the prison. Eventually, somebody asked, "What happened? When did you change? When did you first trust Jesus?"

"The day Brother Tom cried," he answered.

Tears had been all Brother Tom had to offer on the day of which the inmate spoke. The senior Christian envoy to America's prisons had tried every approach he knew. Giving up did not come easily; yet, as thoughts of having to do just that threatened his missionary mind and heart, he began to sob. The tears flowed endlessly for a long time one day as he sat alone with that bitter inmate in his cell.

He had asked for time for just the two of them and there was so much he wanted to say. So much he had planned to say. As it turned out, no words would come but his tears spoke volumes. That day, a man most of society had given up on was changed forever.

Later he would tell Brother Tom, "Nobody ever cried for me before..."

There is much worry about the lack of successful rehabilitation efforts for those presently in our prison systems. Many, on the outside, rant and rave about early release programs for criminals. There does not seem to be enough time, space, or money anymore to arrest and punish everyone who breaks the law.
Those who are prosecuted are eventually released. So there is growing concern about crime and punishment in America. Yes, crimes against society have been committed. And, certainly, those who commit them should pay for their acts. But in some cases a greater crime of omission has been committed against the inmate. There are individuals in our prisons today who have never known the stability and security of a loving home and family...

Of course you can say a few may have been "privileged," There are those who have been given nothing but the best opportunities early in life only to succumb to peer pressure later on. Perhaps one weak moment took them spiraling into gutters dug by drugs and crime.

But many - I dare say, most - have never known, never been told, and never been shown, what real love is all about.

Among these, I suspect, are more than a few who have never seen anybody cry for them. Society has deemed them hopeless and they themselves harbor little cause for hope in their own hearts.

Hope...

<>

Our Histories

The quiet bedroom to which I like to escape is just to the left at the top of the stairs. We'd had a nice toasty fire going in the fireplace and heat had drifted up to warm the entire second floor. In fact it was as warm, if not warmer, than the downstairs rooms when I went up.

Not so when I awoke the next morning. The upstairs heat was off, so I woke up cold. Fingers that were sticking out from under the covers were numb and I couldn't feel my nose. I lay there wondering if the heating system had failed entirely, or if it had just gotten so cold out that the heat pump was no longer performing efficiently. Neither scenario fit.

I had not wakened so cold since I was a kid. I snuggled deep, quickly bringing my numb fingers out twice to slap the snooze button. Finally, I knew I had to crawl out and face the day. I went down the stairs to heavenly warmth and realized I had turned the heat switch off on the upstairs thermostat a couple of weeks back, during the balmy winter 70's, and forgotten to turn it back on.

When I went to bed I had closed the door cutting off all the rising heat from downstairs that had been keeping the area comfortable. Not a heat pump problem, just the controller in error this time.

As I shivered, my heart was flooded with warm memories of childhood and snuggling under the covers with my sister in houses where cold air ruled until daddy or one of my brothers got a fire started in the fireplace.

You'll never see me marching for women's equal rights when it comes to building a fire on a cold morning. I appreciate the men in my life, and I like to have my doors opened for me, and lots of cool stuff that a few narrow-minded feminists decided didn't matter to me.

My cold morning memories were sweet. For many years they were sprinkled with embarrassment and insecurity and a tad of sadness. No more.

Somewhere along the way I came into my own. I learned to like me, really like me, a lot. And when I did, I realized that everything that ever happened to me made me who I am today. Everything I ever had to do without. Every hand-me-down. Every cold morning. Every everything. And I wouldn't trade my past history for anything.

I will never forget spending the day with a Russian physician back in the early 90's. She was about my age and here in the states on some kind of medical exchange program. The day was awesome with lots of modern day cultural dialogue. Assorted food and drink. She drove my husband's tractor, the little orange Kubota he had then, and was unbelievably proud of herself. Heaven only knows how much she would enjoy the John Deere he has now!

It was such a cool day. And then I asked her to tell me about herself. She was confused. She tried to talk about her medical training and her daily duties as a physician and the cultural wealth of her native land.

"No," I said to her, "that's not what I want to hear. I want to know about you, your childhood, your teen years, your marriage ... you."

"My history? MY history ... no one has ever asked about me, wanted to know MY history before." I don't know if she was just trying to accommodate her American host, of if I pulled the plug on a fountain that had needed to erupt for a lifetime. Her native St. Petersburg came to light the way no history book could ever have revealed it to me. I'm not even sure a visit could allow such vision.

After a while she began to share with me many intimate details of her life journey. No, you'll never read about what she said to me in this book or anywhere else. Some words spoken and heard should be held forever in an eternal capsule of time belonging only to the moment which produced them. But some of the memories we think we need to shove back and keep hidden on the other side of yesterday, have a way of finding their rightful place in the future we often call today, and it becomes okay for a brief moment in eternal time to celebrate our history.

< >

REVELATION 3:1-6

*And unto the angel of the church in Sardis write;
These things saith he that hath the seven Spirits of
God, and the seven stars; I know thy works, that thou
hast a name that thou livest, and art dead. Be
watchful, and strengthen the things which remain,
that are ready to die: for I have not found thy works
perfect before God. Remember therefore how thou
hast received and heard, and hold fast, and repent. If
therefore thou shalt not watch, I will come on thee as
a thief, and thou shalt not know what hour I will come
upon thee. Thou hast a few names even in Sardis
which have not defiled their garments; and they shall
walk with me in white: for they are worthy. He that
overcometh, the same shall be clothed in white
raiment; and I will not blot out his name out of the
book of life, but I will confess his name before my
Father, and before his angels. He that hath an ear, let
him hear what the Spirit saith unto the churches.*

A Dream

Unexpectedly, I had reached the end of the road. I stopped my car, and stepped out of the vehicle leaving all my belongings inside. I needed to gain my bearings. I had been traveling for a long, long time. I was weary and now I seemed to have lost my way.

I walked first in one direction and then another. There was no one to be seen although there were signs that others had passed through the area before me, but I was alone. I walked slowly back towards my car. When I topped the hill and looked down into the little valley where I had parked I was startled to find that the car was gone.

I looked all around me. What was happening? It had been no more than 20 to 30 minutes. I had not gone any great distance. Who had taken my car? My purse. My coat. I had none of my belongings with me. No money. Nothing except the clothes on my body. All was gone. I was lost and alone.

Suddenly I saw a light over a hill in the distance, a strange radiance like a combination sunrise and sunset. I walked towards the light. I was puzzled and frustrated.

My things were gone. My life was in my car. The back seat and trunk, even the passenger's seat was full of possessions I would not entrust to the movers. So, I had packed them into my faithful old Ford and headed for my new home. Now, I was alone and lost. I kept walking. Oddly, I was not afraid...

As I topped the hill I gasped to see the most beautiful body of water I had ever beheld. Its crystal brilliance was beyond description. The beach was white and the homes along the shore were grand and stately. All white. There were lots of open windows with billowing white curtains blowing softly in the freedom of a light, refreshing breeze.

As I approached one of the houses that sat near the water's edge, I heard voices. I walked up the steps. Finally, someone would help me! There would be a phone. I would find a way to get back my car and continue on my way.

Feeling an odd freedom to enter without knocking I found that everyone inside was wearing white. Their garments flowed around their bodies in soft elegance. Everyone moved around almost fluidly, with a lightness of being unlike anything I had ever encountered.

My life.
What had happened to my life?
Where was I?

I started to tell my story. My listeners seemed to understand, but no alarm showed on their faces. An unearthly calm prevailed. They told me there was no phone, no going back, and that I should change quickly into my white clothes. Soon it would be time for me to cross the water and I must be dressed for the trip.

Then I awoke.

It was the morning of the seventh anniversary of my father's death.

< >

Healing Tears

The void created by my dad's death is still real and deep. June, 1995 marked my seventh Father's Day without my father. I had been trying to recall those first weeks and months after his death. But I couldn't remember much. The entire first year had become a blur. My telephone bills show there were many long distance calls to my sister. We grieved together over the phone for those first long months. One counselor I talked with told me that was the best way to cope. He said it was good to talk again and again with another who shared the same pain.

He insinuated that I was lucky to have someone who knew how I felt and said such continuing conversation was like repeated debridement of a wound. Each time the wounded area is cleaned it grows smaller as healing occurs from the inside out. I suppose he was right because over time the unbearable became bearable. Yet, to this day, still I can feel his pain and see the anguish in his eyes as my dad fought so hard to live during the last week of his life. He was one of the few for whom open heart surgery did not work the second time.

I lost my mother in 1993, and since early childhood I have grieved often over the deaths of my grandparents, cousins, aunts and uncles. Three grandparents died while I was still in my teens. My paternal grandfather died when I was 23. Several cousins were victims of leukemia and more than a dozen automobile accidents have claimed loved ones. As a nurse, I grew close to many terminally ill patients over the years; they and their families have left indelible imprints upon my heart. Yet, on the day my dad died, I sensed somehow that I would never hurt again any more than I was hurting during the last 12 to 14 hours of his life.

I recall being terribly angry at God, crying out at him from a heart that could not understand how He would allow the sun to shine and daffodils to bloom and all the world to go about business as usual while my father experienced so much pain and anguish. "It should be raining!" I told God. "This day should be dark and dreary, and it should be raining!" All through those last long hours, I prayed. I prayed for a miracle. I prayed for peace. I silently screamed for a sign that God still cared...

I prayed to a God I could not see, hear or feel.
I prayed in anger.
I prayed silently.
I prayed because praying was all I could do.

Only after my father stopped breathing did his pain end.

About an hour after Daddy died, my sister and I left the hospital to go to the hotel and collect our things. We had been asked to come back to sign papers before we headed home. We were told to return through the emergency entrance as all others doors would be locked after midnight.

Shortly before 2 a.m. we drove into the ER parking lot. We sat there for a few minutes, subdued, trying to summon the courage to enter the hospital one more time. I told my sister how I felt about all the early spring flowers that were blooming and how I hated the sunshine which had dared to beam down upon us throughout our five day death vigil.

Tears of reluctant but resolved submission flowed gently.

As we talked of the way Daddy had suffered and of how helpless we had felt to ease his pain, the hearse appeared. It had come to transport my father's body back to his hometown. In that moment, we froze in silence, holding hands, sharing one another's pain, feeling such a terrible and unexplainable void.

As we sat there, tired, still, and alone in the early morning hours, watching the hearse back slowly up to the loading ramp, it started to rain. And I knew, in that instant, that God knew my pain. He had heard my prayers.

Amidst the circumstances of the hour, for whatever reasons forever ink may write, God could do no more than assure me that He knew about our pain.
He knew.
He had heard.
He cared.
And the rain fell for hours...

< >

Dumplings

It was late summer, 1996. Soul food and spirit
vittles was what I needed. Her dumplings were
what I wanted. Though there was/is no
substitute for hers, I attempted to make
dumplings again. Chicken and dumplings, as
well as almost anything chocolate are my
comfort foods. Chocolate reigned solitary until
my mother died in 1993. I miss her. We never
achieved the kind of closeness and friendship I
know we both always wanted.

On the day she lay dying, the charge nurse
called the hospital chaplain to come and visit
with my sister and me. He talked with us for a
couple of hours and prayed for us and for Mary.
That's what he called my mom in his prayer that
day. We were gathered at Mother's bedside
and he prayed for all the kids, and for Mary.
I thought it sounded strange to hear her called
that. She was Mother and she was dying.

Then and now, our grief focused on what could have been. When I miss her, I want chicken and dumplings. (Oh, and her orange cake, I miss it too; but more about that in my Christmas edition of SOUL FOOD and Spirit Vittles.)
What could have been is a doubly sad focus. When regret tinges our memories, the pain seems to sting a little sharper.
Slowly, the years since her death have allowed me to call up good memories of years past, to claim the beauty and joy that comes with those happier, more peaceful times.
As they surface, I find I am able to let go of more and more pain.
It's called healing, I suppose.
It takes time, it is hard, but it is good.
I don't think my dumplings turned out so well. I had made a double batch a few weeks earlier and froze half of the pasty white little rolled and cut squares. Mother did that and her frozen dumplings were always as good as the ones she made fresh. Not so with mine. Mine tasted more like noodles than fat juicy dumplings. And I over-cooked my chicken, too. I had a lot on my mind.

I was at the computer most of the day at one end of my home, the opposite end from where the kitchen is located.

Time got away from me and the chicken cooked a long time.

Too long.

As I write now, it occurs to me that nothing I could have done, or not done, back then, on that sad day, to that effort to make chicken and dumplings could have made the final results perfect.

I think I just missed her too much. It was *her* dumplings I wanted; there was and is no substitute.

You see, a friend who had ALS (Lou Gehrig's disease) had called me the day before to tell me his case manager had told him it would soon be the end.

"The end?" I asked. "The end of what? The study program? The end of the experimental drug therapy?"

"No, the end of my life," he said.

I started to sob. ALS is cruel. It robs you of all strength and takes away your ability to function in every way we come to know as normal.

I disintegrated emotionally. After we hung up, I continued to cry uncontrollably for a very long time. I went to the bathroom, turned on the shower, stepped into the erasing flow and stayed there until both the hot water and tears stopped flowing.

That night, I called my friend back to apologize for losing my composure on the phone with him earlier.

He assured me no apology was necessary.

I told him I was angry, downright mad, and that I felt helpless.

He told me not to worry, that God was in control.

"In control?" I wondered silently.

I suppose he heard my thoughts.

He continued, "I reckon I have always felt like God was in control, in the good times and the bad. Even when I thought I was in control, I suppose I know now that He was, and still is."

It was the next morning when I went to the grocery to buy the chicken. I cooked the critter all day long. I only wanted to beat the walls and scream, but I cooked chicken. My friend said my chicken and dumplings were "pretty darn good."

<>

Amazing Grace

It was 1997, the beginning of another year. Normally, as a new year begins I am a bit more self-centered.

Normally, I would be thinking of all the things I need to do to improve myself; considering what I can do to enhance relationships with family and friends; planning a bit more intensely, contemplating how I could improve production at work; gathering information for tax time.

Normally, I would be doing any number of things, except pondering on God's Amazing Grace like I was back in the early days of 1997.

How marvelously sweet the sound!
How incomprehensible!
How phenomenal!
I fear to think, to try to imagine, or begin to comprehend where we all would be without God's truly Amazing Grace!

Normal is not a word I could apply to that present moment or to any of the thoughts that were dancing in and out of my mind and heart.

A friend was dying and my heart was breaking. It's not like it was a surprise.

You are just never ready to let death take a loved one.

Oh, you may say you are ... sometimes, the pain and suffering becomes so intense that you pray for a release.

You pray for rest.
For sleep that won't come.
Mostly, you pray for peace, for the kind of calm that always accompanies any measure of God's Amazing Grace.
You pray for it in abundance.
And when it comes you marvel.

That's all you can do.

You simply marvel.

I once wrote a little poem that I thought was a
bit too simplistic at the time the ink was flowing
onto the paper.
Childlike, I thought. Almost kindergartenish!

> Jesus loves us,
> this I know
> why He loves us,
> I don't know
> but, tell me,
> what more
> do we need to know?

Sometimes, however, such truth seems utterly
profound and I find it is all I need to know.
Shortly after the weakness began to take its toll,
my husband took our friend canoeing down the
Ocmulgee River.

I never heard a grown man talk about anything
on earth with such awe, such total rapture, as he
did when he spoke afterwards of the experience.
The trip was one of those things he had always
thought he might do if he ever had the time.

Our friend had worked for a major airline for nearly thirty years.

He also owned a quite successful landscaping business.

He had a beautiful wife, two children and a dog. He loved his life. He had no complaints.

Really, he had no complaints...

He was kind of quiet, not really shy, just quieter than most.

He believed in hard work and honesty.

A man of principles, devoted to family and friendship.

And, oh, how he had always enjoyed the beauty and calm of the outdoors.

But work and family obligations had kept him from doing some of the things he had always thought he might do if he ever had the time.

As his wife sat on the edge of their bed, while the end neared, her head throbbing, eyes swollen, tears flowing, she kept whispering softly, "He doesn't deserve to suffer like this..."

No, I thought, he doesn't deserve the inescapable agony that accompanies Lou Gehrig's Disease at any stage and especially in the last months. No one does.

And then I remembered the one thing that makes times like this bearable:

Jesus loves us.

He loved us enough to die for us, to die alone that we may never be alone in life, or in death. As he struggled so miserably for air and rest, I whispered to my friend "Whenever it gets bad like this, whenever you start to feel the panic, just let yourself float down the river again; but this time, leave my husband behind and let Jesus handle the oars. Rest and float and see the sights with Jesus as your Guide."

I thought even as the words rolled too smoothly off my tongue, "How simplistic, how easy for you to say..."

But the next morning as I pondered the loss we would soon know, I realized my words were not so simplistic after all.

I remembered that storm so many long years ago in which the disciples feared for their lives while their master slept.

When their panic forced them to wake Him and express their fears, He calmly spoke three words that would change forever the course, not only of that little boat, but of their lives and mine,

"Peace, be still ..."

I suspected that Jesus, Master of all the stormy waters of our lives, surely can manage another majestic canoe ride down the Ocmulgee, and/or all the other rivers of our lives, until we eventually cross the Jordan.

God's Amazing Grace assured me then and now that He can.

<>

PSALM 119:169

Let my cry come near before thee, O Lord:
give me understanding according to thy word.

Confronting Death

It was one week after my friend had died.
After he drew his last breath, within a short span
of minutes, maybe an hour or two, any number
of spoken phrases danced in and out of my
consciousness.

"He is in a better place."
"He is better off."
"Heaven has another angel now."
"He doesn't have to suffer anymore."
Etc. Etc. Etc.

Yet, all I could feel, think, and say is, "My friend is
gone."
At some point, I thought perhaps I could consider
more readily what was best for him.
But right then I could only feel a tremendous loss.
It was a wonderful hospice program in which he
was enrolled.
Enrolled?
Yes, I suppose that is as good a choice of words
as any.
He chose the hospice route, so I suppose I can
say he enrolled himself in their program.

Yet, it was not their program, but his own which he followed.

He called the shots.

The social workers, nurses, sitters, volunteers and all who were involved in his life over the last six or seven months were there to make him as comfortable as possible, to meet all needs that could be met.

They did what they were called upon to do beautifully, lovingly, and tenderly.

My friend had opted early on in his battle with Lou Gehrig's Disease not to have a tracheostomy, feeding tubes, intravenous feedings or any heroic resuscitation measures once the end loomed near.

He chose instead to live well only the days that were his to live "normally."

During the summer and early fall, he had attended all of his son's ball games; he even traveled with the team to the playoffs.

He pushed himself to be there to watch, to silently cheer, to enjoy his son's activities.

Then every weekend, beginning in October, long time buddies had driven him to the hunting camp he had shared with them for more than twenty years.

They built a ramp for his wheelchair, set up a generator for his oxygen and put a comfortable recliner in place so he could be where he wanted to be and do what he wanted to do with as much ease as possible.

I remember clearly how depressed he was in January of '96, so certain was he at that point that he would never get to enjoy another hunting season.

Not that hunting mattered so much to him. Instead, it was being close to nature, "to God," he would say, "to the camaraderie and the camp fire."

Nobody has ever enjoyed a camp fire quite like my friend did.

On a Sunday evening, only a few weeks before his death we had him down at our farm.

Long after the wieners and marshmallows were toasted and tasted, well after all the stars had come out and even after those of us who had to go to work the next morning had begun counting the hours till dawn, my friend wanted "one more log" thrown on the fire.

He taught us much about beauty and patience. He never complained.

He never asked "Why me?"

At times he was frustrated when he would be "ready to go" and, for some reason, his illness would level off again and he would realize it wasn't time yet.

But he learned to go with the flow and to bask in the glow from the fading flame of his earth life. Only during his last few weeks did the tears begin to come during our conversations; but they never overshadowed his sense of humor, optimism and love of life.

On the contrary, his tears, his personal grief over his own physical demise, only seemed to cleanse him of any imperfections that remained. I have come to believe that such poignantly timed tears are quite healing to our spirit.

My friend and others like him were the reason I most enjoyed nursing.

He and they were also one reason I do not regret leaving the profession.

The dying became too hard.

In many cases, terminally ill individuals are afforded the time to learn to accept.

We who minister to them often are too busy to learn to accept.

The pain is compounded with each loss.

Sometimes it gets to be a bit much.

Yet, it is from the dying that I have learned the most invaluable lessons about living.

We are the lucky ones who cross their paths as they grasp the true meanings of perspective, reality and life.

When they sprinkle a bit of truth's dust at our feet, we must find the courage to walk forward in it.

But more than finding the courage to walk on, we must take the time to slow down, throw "one more log" on the fire and enjoy the golden flame of life with those we love before it's too late.

< >

Heaven - Eternity - Tomorrow

Following the loss of a loved one, our thoughts
frequently are of the hereafter.
What it is like where they have gone?
How does it happen - the transition?
How different is the next life from the one here
on earth?
What will life be like in that other realm?
In this realm, on this side of eternity, our hearts
ache. And, sometimes, we cry because we
cannot understand why we must wait, why hate
reigns in a world that should know better, why
prejudicial chains bind hearts that would be free
if freedom were only the choice!
Indeed, ours is a lovely, but imperfect world.
As if our cultural and geographical divisions are
not enough, we oft times withdraw to corners of
our own private worlds to erect more walls, real
and imaginary, which further separate us from
our fellowman.
Will the separation end in Heaven? Will we
come together at last when we are in the
presence of One Whose love longs to destroy
the most fortified defense systems of mankind in
a determined effort to save us from ourselves?

Heaven? Streets of gold have never held any particular fascination for me. Actually, I cannot think of anything less inviting. Instead, I hope there will be clear, bubbling streams which ripple and hum like those which flow through my beloved north Georgia mountains. And I imagine there must be trees in Heaven – trees like the vanishing old South Georgia water oak whose massive limbs filter light from a sky almost as blue as Montana's. And flowers that bloom eternally while birds sing of everlasting peace. Ah, yes, I have high hopes for heaven, but golden streets just aren't among them. Indeed, I have many ideas about Heaven – many expectations, but, trust me, I'm not interested in anything gold.

More than all else I long to be in the presence of One Whose love has climbed the highest mountains, walked the longest valleys, crossed the most barren deserts, forded the widest oceans and destroyed the most fortified barrier erected by mankind in a determined effort to save us from ourselves. One Whose Love never fails. It is a love that will reign supreme when tomorrow comes. I truly believe this. My faith tells me I can.

< >

Faith, huh?

It was a long time ago and I sat pondering once more the meaning of faith, and once again was coming up void of any fine and fancy definitions. Expectation?
Hope?
Trust?
These and other ordinary words we associate with faith popped into mind, yet I was at a loss for personalizing the definition that day.
I remember it like it was yesterday.
The phone rang and it was my sister, Lynda, the one who was in the insurance business at the time and who always has an answer for everything.
Well, almost always...
"What is faith?" I asked her.
You wouldn't believe her answer. She went on and on! The stories and examples and explanations she spits out, then and now, are endless. It's amazing. Absolutely amazing! And more often than I care to admit, she's on the mark. When one of her dissertations is over I am usually unresponsive, like I chose to be that day. I had known better than to ask.
"Are you there," she said?

"Umm hmm, but I don't have a lot of faith."

"I know. You never have had. You've always felt like you had to do everything. It's that oldest child syndrome."

"But Lynda, I am supposed to speak at a Kiwanis club breakfast in the morning on the subject of faith."

"Oh, no," she gasped, "why you?"

"Well, folks who read my column must think I have a lot of faith, so I reckon that's why I got invited."

"Well, you don't," she said, "You never have had. But I gotta give it to you, you know well the God in whom you have what little faith you do own up to. In fact, I have often wondered what would happen if folks who know God like you do ever learned how to act in total faith - that kind the Bible says will move a mountain. You probably could move them, you know, I mean really, literally move them!"

"Then why does it seem like I'm always climbing them instead of moving them?"

"Maybe you were just meant to be a mountain climber. Faith is a gift you know."

"I know that. And I want more than I have."

"Why?"

"Why not?"

"Why do you want more faith? Answer me."
"Cause it would make things easier."
"No it wouldn't."
"Yes, it would."
"I have a lot of faith. My faith puts yours to shame. Do you think my life is any easier than yours?"
"Is this a trick question?"
"What do you think?"
"About what?"
"Do you think my life is any easier than yours because I have more faith?"
Assuredly, I was evading that one.
No, her life was not any easier than mine and I knew it, but I was not going to give her the satisfaction of hearing me say it aloud.
I was toying with the idea of having a pity party someday soon and I got the impression she was trying to deny me the pleasure.

"You are not going to answer me are you," she continued.
Badgering is what she was doing.

Obliging her with an occasional grunt, I stood up with phone in hand and stepped gingerly across my office floor (laden with papers and books and coloring crayons – my grandson had spent the afternoon with me). I walked to the end of the room where my favorite posters grace the wall. I was about to reach to take down the poster of the girl in the swing with The Big Hand reaching out to her and the caption that said, "Will you trust Me?"

"What are you doing? Are you there?"

"Oh, no!" I gasped. "It's gone!"

"What's gone?"

"The poster I was going to use in the morning to launch my little talk on faith. It's not here!"

"What did it say?"

"Will you trust me?"

"I do trust you."

"No, silly, the poster. The poster was a picture of God's hand reaching out to a girl precariously perched in a swing. Across the top were the words, "Will you trust me?"

"Well, will you?" she said.

See what I mean?

Again, I had no response for her.

I hung up the phone and recalled the words recorded in small print at the bottom of the missing poster:

"Trust in the Lord with all thine heart
and lean not unto thine own understanding,
in all thy ways acknowledge Him
and He shall direct Thy paths."

I suspected it was that "all thine heart" part that holds the key to defining faith.
My faith is deeper now, but I still struggle.
My experiences may differ somewhat from yours.
Your path and/or circumstances may be foreign to me, as mine would be to you.
Yet, I suspect there is a common chord between us – a chord of faith.
Yes, faith, that "substance of things hoped for and evidence of things not seen," according to the writer of the New Testament Book of Hebrews.
Webster has defined faith as firm belief in something for which there is no proof.
Belief, confidence, or conviction may be synonymous as well.
Yet, no matter what definition I go with, sometimes I run low on the stuff.

I recall how an afternoon eclipse of the sun in 1991 made me wonder, "Does God slip out of sight and hide His face from us as easily as the sun or moon or stars?"

Over time, I have come to know that He does not.

The circumstances in which we find ourselves on occasion may lend creditability to our suspicions that He does.

There may be times when it is not possible to see His hand at work or to feel His presence in our day-to-day lives, but no, God does not hide from us His face, His love, the work of His hands, or anything that is the essence of Who and What He is.

Once, during an especially trying time, when I was quite certain God had exited the scene, I spoke with a friend about the terrible apprehensions I was experiencing and how I had just about exhausted my very limited supply of faith.

She responded, "How can your faith be limited? My faith is all I have!"

"Give me a break!" I thought, "That's what you get for thinking somebody might understand!"

There I was pouring out my heart, talking about all my troubles and telling her my faith was about gone when she goes and brags about it being all she's got!

I listened long to her go on and on about her inexhaustible supply of faith.

At one point she looked me squarely in the eye, a lot like my sister might, and said, "I just don't understand comments like that from someone like you. I am sure you pray and that's all it takes to have faith."

"Please don't expect me to buy that," I thought again, but I had the good sense not to say it aloud.

As I walked away, my little voice whispered, "She's right you know. When have you prayed?"

In his letter to the Hebrews, I think it was Paul who defined faith as "the assurance of things hoped for, the conviction of things not seen." That word "things" has always bothered me. Language can be so limiting.

Maybe there was no better word than "things" to lead off with in that first verse of the eleventh chapter of Hebrews.

But I think the rest of the chapter gives us a reasonable understanding of the concept of faith.

It's sad that we so often focus on things when we talk to God in prayer. We set our minds and hearts on certain goals, accomplishments, relationships or "things" and we pray for those desires. I'm not sure that's the wisest approach to enhancing our relationship with our Heavenly Father or the most effective way to participate in the miracle of prayer.

Too many times we pray for things that we do not receive from God.

We may even fast and pray.

We may claim to have faith that God will answer our prayers and give us the desires of our hearts. Yet, our prayers supposedly go unanswered if we consider that most of us have trouble accepting "NO" as an answer.

When considering the subjects of faith and prayer I have many ideas and notions about how God involves Himself in the affairs of mankind.

I have no concept of a God Who constantly interferes in our affairs, making things turn out just the way we want them to, or the way He wants them to.

That kind of reasoning or believing is far from me.

What I do believe is that God is always aware of what's going on with His children and that He cares deeply, rejoicing with us over our victories, grieving with us when we face defeat or failure, standing ever ready to give us great wealth from His storehouse of spiritual gifts.

Then what we do with those spiritual gifts is almost entirely up to us.

What greater responsibility is there than to get to know ourselves?

To learn from our many experiences? To recognize and use the spiritual gifts bestowed upon us? To develop our mind and body?

To choose to become all we are capable of becoming for the good of our fellowman?

To have a purpose that will matter for all eternity?

That's right, all eternity. Nothing will ever convince me that life stops at the grave or at the "end" as we sometimes refer to the death of the body in which we live on earth.

Not only do our works live on after we are gone from this place, but our souls lives on in the place to which we go.

Walking with God, believing He is near, knowing His presence is with us is a great thing.

It makes for peace of mind like nothing else can. There is no greater security. Such awareness, however, does not relieve you or me of the responsibility for making our own choices. Circumstances in which we find ourselves may sometimes be totally beyond our control; but, our reaction to those circumstances is within our control. There may be occasions when we have little or no choice about the people whose company we must keep for long or short periods of time, as well as occasions when we have little control over illness and misfortune that strikes ... goals that become unreachable ... dreams that fade ... the fact that those who are so dear to us, go or grow away from us; but, always we have the power to choose how we will react to the parade of circumstances which march before us along the highway of life.

There was indeed a time when I thought a great deal about faith and felt that I just didn't have quite enough.

Now, I don't think much about the subject of faith. I think about God and I think about life.

I think about how exciting it is to be living with a deep awareness that God loves us and how wonderful it is to know that we are never alone.

It's vital that we live one day at a time, one hour at a time, even one minute at a time!

And it's important to realize that sometimes, in spite of our best efforts, we will fall short of set goals, we will miss opportunities that we think we should not have missed, and we will fail when we were so sure we were going to succeed.

In other words, sometimes, we are simply going to blow it! I'm sure you can relate.

Our triumphs and successes bound together with our blunders and failures are an integral part of the university of life where we are learning more about ourselves and our Creator.

Amidst this continuous acquisition of knowledge, and hopefully wisdom as well, perhaps it is faith that enables us to choose to live fully and completely, not only for today, but for all of eternity.

< >

Strange are the things
that can become the straw,
the one that breaks the camel's back, that is.
Usually, we know
when we are getting too near the edge,
when our limit has been reached,
when we have had all we can stand.
There are signs, hints.
We have warnings.
and when we have those warnings,
if we are wise, we back off.
We will allow ourselves a quiet time,
a time to ask:
"What does it all matter in the light of eternity?"
< >

This present moment is a good moment. Claim it. Look out a window. Watch a child at play. Hold a baby. Forget skin color. Forget age. Forget ability or inability. Try to see a bright red cardinal in a naked tree for the first time. Let yourself listen to the rhythm of the rain. Touch someone's hand. Smile at a stranger. Hug a loved one. Hug hard and long. Attempt to look into the hearts of those with whom you live, work or play. Listen to what they say and don't say (in their silence you will hear much). Allow yourself to recognize traits in others for which you can be thankful. Acknowledge and accept those traits within yourself as well. They are there. Be willing to see things in new ways. It can be a season of the year, a song, a deep conversation with a friend or a quick exchange with a stranger that prompts my introspection and yours. Let it take you where it will. Don't be afraid to remember, to ponder, to think and feel deeply. As you recall so much of what has made you who you are today, allow yourself to cultivate a spirit of thanksgiving. Permit new insight. Allow for a change of mind. Let yourself see the Hand of God as it has gently pointed, nudged, even reprimanded. It's okay to just be... to just BE in the present moment called today.

<>

The Next Place

I could not hush talking about the book for hours. Of course, for the first few minutes, I was speechless. Tears had begun to trickle down my cheeks before I was half through turning the beautiful pages. It was strange how the impact of the words held me frozen for an instant somewhere in past or future time.

Once I regained my composure I began talking to all around me about the glorious little book, and here I am still talking about it. A young man who had witnessed my immediate reaction asked to see it.

As he started to flip through the pages, I cautioned him, "That is not a book to flip through. You should savor every page, slowly." Laid out like a children's book, "The Next Place" appeals to the sense of wonder in all of us - wonder, that is, about the afterlife. It deserves a slow flipping of its pages.

The young man attempted to do what I suggested and then commented that it was hard to follow. He was referring to the way the words waltz across the pages of sunrises and sunsets, stars and moons, and delicate birds that beckon one to fly with them into the unknown.

"Sir, have you ever lost a loved one?" I asked.

"What do you mean?" he responded.

"I mean, has anyone close to you, someone you cared deeply about, ever died?" I asked.

"No," he said.

"Then close the book, but buy it and save it until you lose someone. Only then you will be able to appreciate the pages you are holding," I said in amazement.

It always shocks me when an adult of any age tells me that death has never claimed a loved one.

Of course, having come from a very large family, I suppose my chances of knowing loss early on were far greater than in those families of recent decades where two kids have been the limit. It is with great clarity that I recall the first death I ever witnessed. My cousin William was nine years old when leukemia took his life. I was two. The extended family (my mom was one of eleven children) had gathered at the home to support the immediate family in the last days and hours of William's earth's presence.

They probably thought I was too small to know what was going on. Not so. It may have been on that day that my quest began to try to understand what follows after. It had only been twenty-four months since I had left what comes before. Maybe I was still young enough and open enough to realize they may be one and the same.

In my quest to learn more about "The Next Place" I was told that some Texan who read it wrote the publisher to protest the author's attempt to contemplate the afterlife. Can you believe that? On the other hand, ordained minister Della Reese, also the star of the highly successful CBS series "Touched by an Angel," ordered copies for her entire congregation after she read the little book.

"The Next Place" was published in 1997. At hundreds of signings around the country families and friends who have lost loved ones have thanked author and illustrator Warren Hanson for his lovely work of art.

Strangely, the book is not religious at all. There is no mention of God. Thus I have found it odd that it has so captivated me and others. Odd, that is, until I remembered the words of Paul in his first chapter of the book of Romans. I was reminded that those who want to see God will see Him in everything. Those who do not may see Him in nothing. And so I saw God on every page of "The Next Place."

From "The Next Place:"

I won't remember getting there.
Somehow I'll just arrive.
But I'll know that I belong there
and I will feel much more alive
than I have ever felt before.
I will be absolutely free
of the things I held onto
that were holding onto me...

Excerpted with permission from Waldman House Press, the same publisher who brought us "A Cup of Christmas Tea" and so many great and exquisitely beautiful inspirational books. Waldman House books are available through any book store and many gift shops.

< >

Does Eternity Matter NOW?

Sometimes it amazes me, even intimidates me a bit, when I pause to realize how open I am with you on the printed page.

When I started writing in 1986, my objectives were few. Certainly I wanted to continue to promote health and healing. Having been a nurse for more than a decade, I'd had many opportunities to observe how physical pain could often be more easily addressed than what I came to recognize as "the pain behind the pain." I decided that encouraging better communication would be one way to try to help alleviate that very dangerous and debilitating subdued pain.

Communicating openly myself was a way to begin. In the early years, my newspaper column was dubbed "From the heart..." I don't rightly remember when editors dropped that and just started putting my name with a headline of sorts. Doesn't matter, a rose is still a rose and I still write from the heart, which is the way I encourage others to communicate.

Have I succeeded? Only time will tell. Might take all of eternity. That's okay. I'll be around. And that brings me to another reason I write.

I want folks to look for an eternal perspective in all things. Hard to see, huh? Maybe. But, with issues of real importance, the eternal perspective is there. Note I did not say urgent issues. There is so often a tremendous difference between urgence and importance. Recognizing the difference between the two must be a top priority if we would have our lives count for eternity.

And what does eternity matter? Why can't I just believe the here and now is all there is?

Since early childhood, I have given that question much thought. I have concluded that for those who follow after us on planet earth, we make a difference either way. History's influence is ever felt. I cannot prove there is a tomorrow beyond the grave, but I choose to live my life with that eternal perspective. In my heart, I know God is real.

That brings me to another reason I write, which is to tell others how much God loves them. There is no greater message. Never has been. Never will be. There is no limiting the person who knows he or she is loved.

Love lifts, motivates, empowers!

When we are loved, and know it, we are healthier and happier. Even a new born baby responds positively to love. You may say it's easier for an infant since they have not been as traumatized, disillusioned or hurt. Get real! After nine months of warmth and safety, cuddled in the womb and cushioned from the impact of the world, birth takes place. It has to be a rude awakening. But, when the birthing is over, it is downright awesome to observe an infant's response to the loving caress of a mother, father or another compassionate caregiver.

It is never too late for someone to respond positively to being loved. Oh, I know there are many who would argue with me about that one. "Just check out the prison population," I've been told more times than I care to remember. "Look at politics," they say. And, "you think there is redemption for the corporate world?" I am often asked. I'm not sure I understand all the queries I get, but I do understand love. God's love.

I did not always get it. I think the tide turned for me the first time I met someone who loved me unconditionally. She was practically a stranger when she first invited me to her home for a Thursday morning bible study. There was something different about her from the very beginning. There was an acceptance. There were no expectations on her part about what I should think, believe or "know."

When I entered her presence, my forever questioning heart, soul and mind were welcomed right along with the rest of me. It was God in her who loved me. It took a while to realize it. In fact, it was the day we buried her that full realization began to set in. I've not been the same since.

So profound were the revelations that began to come my way, following my exposure to the unconditional love of God so actively demonstrated through Maxine Carter, that I cannot keep them to myself. Writing is a relatively comfortable platform from which I can share some of them. And so I write. It's been a while since I thanked you for reading.

Thank you!

<>

Grief

I have attempted, on occasion, to write special poems for special people, sometimes by request and sometimes just because I wanted to reach out in any way I knew how. Perhaps it is a need within myself which prompts me to offer encouragement through the written word. There is always a trade-off, for I have found that as I give, I receive.

It may be a few verses of Scripture, a timely note or a short poem which gently speaks hope to one who is hurting too badly to venture out of his or her private little world in search of relief from misery they deem to be theirs alone.

Grief and the strong sense of failure or intense frustration that accompanies the inevitable bedfellow, will often forbid that we venture outside of ourselves for a time when it is fresh. We are made to recoil. We long to hide from the storms which beat upon us. Devastating experiences can make emotional cripples of otherwise healthy individuals. Often, painful circumstances can render one incapable of believing that life will ever be better again.

Sure, there are many good, even great, books to be read and a wide variety of resources to be found; but we have to be ready. We must move beyond that initial shock of intense loss before we can choose to seek help if we need it. And I dare say most of us need help from time to time.

So, I write for me and for you. We may have known pain in different forms, for different reasons, and in different worlds. Our common bond, however, is the need to know that there will be a tomorrow when we will feel better once more, a tomorrow when recent tragedies will no longer reign like a heavy, dark cloud which refuses to ever allow the sun to shine in our lives again, a tomorrow when we can let go of yesterday's pain.

< >

Remembrances Matter

We all seek to hold onto the magic moments of our lives, to hide them for a season, in the corners of our hearts.

Even as it is poured upon us, we try to stash a measure of the joy in which time does not permit us to revel. We attempt to gather and file many of the little happinesses that are sprinkled along our paths; we claim we want to save them for a time when we can savor them. We take photographs. We keep journals. We store well the highlights of our days.

We say we live for the day when we can *relive* those precious moments in which our hearts were warmed and our souls refreshed.

We must take care - as we imagine ourselves curled up in tomorrow's favorite easy chair, before a glowing winter fire, hot chocolate in hand, relishing anew the joys of the spring times of our lives - indeed, we must take care that these remembrances are not usurped by some tragedy, loss, or pain which demands equal space in our memory banks.

The memories we make when tragedy strikes, pain hits, or loved ones are lost - those memories, too, must find their rightful place in the figuratively heart shaped storage center of our lives.

We have no choice but to let them in, and frequently we do so with a certain resolve to never pull them up again. We want painful memories out of sight and out of mind, and so we file them away to collect dangerous dust next to the other private annals of our souls.

Time goes by.

We live with full awareness that if we are to ever again access the joy we stashed there we must come face to face with the sadness that also lurks in the shadowy places of our hearts. And so we stay busy. We seek diversions. In our leisure, we dance in the embrace of cowardice. We start to lose ourselves.

To refuse to go again into the dark corners of our hearts, pull back the curtains of the soul and let the sunshine in on all that we are, have been, or ever hope to be, is to refuse to live!

For it is in these hidden places that the very essence of life is stored. Fear not to take regular inventory. Acknowledge the presence of all that rests there. Appreciate the balance that will evolve. Celebrate the vision that will become uniquely your own. Accept the peace that comes as you discover the truth time alone can teach - truth hidden in the corners of your heart.

I once read part of what I have written here to my ten-year-old niece to see if she could comprehend what I am trying to say. "I think I get it," she said. "It's like on Diagnosis Murder, when this girl's best friend was killed. She couldn't let herself think of her friend at all because it made her so sad. But before the sad thing happened there was lots of fun and she couldn't think about the fun times either."

Yep.

Please don't think I am saying it's not okay to deny things for a while when tragedy strikes. Denial can serve us well for a season, but only for a season. Denial, carried to extremes, however, can rob us of much that we should keep and treasure.

A broken marriage, crumbled friendship, the loss of one's health, and a great many catastrophic events leave us no choice at times but to recoil. We find we must deny until we can cope better; actually, denial is a form of coping. I know there are some things that need to be buried and never resurrected again; but be careful when you do that. Be careful that the burial ground does not lie between you and the many treasures you do want to dig up at some later date.

Life is meant to be lived, lived fully and completely, and if you are lucky enough to make it to that easy chair by the fire one day, do not hesitate to relive the highlights and the lowlights.

Most remembrances, even the sad ones, bring with them a measure of wisdom and joy - maybe even a giggle or two! And unlike so many of life's other so-called treasures, those stashed in the corners of our hearts cannot be taken from us. Just be careful what you put there. You have more control over such matters than you think you do.

< >

On November 8, 1966, a fellow nursing student shared with me the following words which I recorded on a blank page separating the Old and New Testament in what is now my oldest and very worn Bible. I regret I do not know the origin of these words which I now share with you.

"Once I fit together the bits, pieces, hopes, fears and desires that make me the person I am, I hope to have the courage to act on my discoveries and follow them through.
The adventure will be well worth the quest.
Once I find a pattern of life so absorbing that I lose myself in it then I will find myself."

The adventure has indeed proven well worth the quest. That student sharing those words with me back then has played a direct role in the sharing of my words with you today. For so flows the river of life. In losing myself to such flow, I have indeed found myself and so much more.

< >

II SAMUEL 12:16-23

David therefore besought God for the child; and David fasted, and went in, and lay all night upon the earth. And the elders of his house arose, and went to him, to raise him up from the earth: but he would not, neither did he eat bread with them. And it came to pass on the seventh day, that the child died. And the servants of David feared to tell him that the child was dead: for they said, Behold, while the child was yet alive, we spake unto him, and he would not hearken unto our voice: how will he then vex himself, if we tell him that the child is dead? But when David saw that his servants whispered, David perceived that the child was dead: therefore David said unto his servants, Is the child dead? And they said, He is dead. Then David arose from the earth, and washed, and anointed himself, and changed his apparel, and came into the house of the Lord, and worshipped: then he came to his own house; and when he required, they set bread before him, and he did eat. Then said his servants unto him, What thing is this that thou hast done, thou didst fast and weep for the child, while it was alive; but when the child was dead, thou didst rise and eat bread. And he said, While the child was yet alive, I fasted and wept: for I said, Who can tell whether God will be gracious to me, that the child may live? But now he is dead, wherefore should I fast? can I bring him back again? I shall go to him, but he shall not return to me.

Tomorrow Calls

Tomorrow calls
and our destination beckons.
Yet, to meander down memory lane
and pause for a moment or two
at the doorway of yesterday
is a luxury we can ill afford to turn down.

Alas! To walk through that door again
is forbidden now.
Though it was the chosen road back then
we shall travel it no more,
except in memory.

Oh! There will always be those September days
when we will recall the many paths
which once lay before us,
and the choices we made,
and the voices we heard calling us,
voices which still may softly call today
Ah, yes! Tomorrow!

Where an untraveled path awaits those
who would keep on traveling
dauntless and unafraid,
knowing the price they paid
will be worth it all
when tomorrow comes.

When all the regrets of yesterday
have seemed to fade
into the grandest sunset of all the ages,
tomorrow will come
and the sun will shine
on a new day,
a day in which we will, at last
see as we are even now seen
and know as we have always been known
a day when we will have reached our
destination
and
finally found our way back home.
< >

PSALM 34:18

The Lord is nigh unto them that are of a broken heart; and saveth such as be of a contrite spirit.

Cry Not For Me

Cry not for me in the dark hour
for like the window of my youth
death shall be but a window through which
I shall climb at the appointed time
so that I might slip away
on my continued quest
for knowledge of that One
I first sought to know so long ago.
Think not that death's momentary
darkness shall defeat you
Victory will be yours, too
for, somewhere, the stars shine
and I among them shall shine for you.
I shall help to light the night
for you to see how to come to me
when it is right for you to follow.
So, fear not the journey ahead.
Simply trust that it was right
for me to go before you and know
that I shall wait on the other side
with arms open wide to welcome you
to bid you enter into the eternal glory
that is ours to share with God
forever and ever and for all time.

<>

There is Tomorrow

There is tomorrow.
Oh, yes! There is a tomorrow.

Though sometimes,
when loved ones are gone
and death seems to have had the final say
we are left to wonder
how we can go on this way
day after day
with only the memories
of laughter
and of children at play
to haunt the empty rooms
of the lives we're tempted
to feel might have been wasted
ever mindful of the joy it seems we barely
tasted when there was only yesterday.

And we wonder if she left all cares behind
or if he shares the pain of the void
created by her leaving
or if grieving
is a thing unknown
in the world to which she or he has gone.

And, too, we wonder anew
as the past unfolds once more
why it was she who had to go before us
and not we,
why we could not be there
to take his hand and
lead the way
as we had done so many times
along the path of yesteryear.
And as a tear freely flows
it is as though God personally
knows the lonely anguish
of each and every room.
As we feel Him draw near,
we hear again the echo
of the empty tomb
as the gentle promise
of all the ages permits
the time-honored message
of peace and everlasting hope
to permeate the places
of our deepest pain and sorrow
so that we may know there is tomorrow.
Indeed! There is a tomorrow!

< >

Henceforth, I shall value only that which I can take with me when I die and that is only what I give away.

Claim Your Grief

When the sun comes up
on that grand tomorrow
every tear
will have been washed away
and your long silent heart
will sing one more time
but I know
tomorrow seems aeons away.
So you must claim
today's brief melancholy
and waste not
the great truths it shall teach
for there are times in life when
the only solace there is
is that which comes from knowing
you are not alone in your grief.

< >

Letting Go

The world lies before me
and I pause   knowing
I must live out today
ere I shall gain entrance
into Tomorrow's Land.
Like unto the sorrow
which comes with the release
of a loved one's hand
when he makes his final
exit from this place
is the pain I feel today.
Reluctance reigns.
Within, there is a heavy fullness;
without, only emptiness
and with the rise
and fall of my breast
there is an exchange
until I no longer know
what is empty and what is full,
but I do know
that the world lies before me
and my pause at this threshold
of tomorrow must be brief.

I must move forward
and Life must be lived.
To live life well today
is the greatest tribute
I can pay to those
who wait for me
in Tomorrow's Land,
those who have gone
before me
         to blaze the trail
                  and to make a way
                           for me to follow them
                                             some day.
                                             < >

Corners of my Heart

There are tiny corners of my heart
where pain resides
and hurt hides

There are dark shadows in my mind
where doubts abound
and fear is found

There's disappointment at every turn
when friends fail
and dreams fade

Frustration!
Sorrow!
Anger!
Flood my being!
My eyes never seeing
Beyond myself.

Blinded by tears of self-centered anguish,
Unable to free myself
From the quicksands of this world,

Too tired to stand
Too weak to make demands,
Too broken to care.
I bow at last my proud head
and pray
"Father, not my will, but Thine."

Then Peace comes!
Joy Follows!
And Laughter hides just around the bend!

And the feet which could not move
suddenly want to run toward Life
and all its challenges
For God is with me
and with His eyes I see
I can run when I am weary
I can walk and not faint.
The fire will not encompass me!
The floods will not overwhelm me!
The rocks will be moved
and my path made straight!

I shall enter!

I shall enter!

I shall enter!

Thru that narrowest of gates,

I shall stand in His presence

I shall bow at His name

And the half has never been told
of His Grace
of His glory
of His majesty
and of how His very presence
led me all the way!

< >

I Lived!

I lived to laugh
and cry
and wonder why
and wait
until
another day
to die
then live again
to never cry
alone again
to only smile
and sigh
to know that
"why"?
does not matter
anymore
< >

Awake!

With the dawning of every new day
comes an opportunity
"to begin again"
Do not thoughtlessly
throw that chance away
by clinging to
yesterday's pain.

Let Go and Live!
< >

A Note of Thanks

Many thanks to all my fellow warrior maidens
who fight to feed because
they know and understand the need for
SOUL FOOD and Spirit Vittles.
I love doing life with you!
A few feeding names dancing thru my mind and heart today are
Agnes
Amanda, Andrea, Angy, Ann, Ashley, Aubree
Barbara, Betsy, Betty, Bonnie, Brenda, Catherine, Charlie, Charlynn
Chelsea, Cherie, Chonda, Colleen, Cynthia, Dana, Daniele, Debra
Deeba, Diane, Diliana, Elise, Glenna, Gloria, Haley Harleigh, Harriet
Ina, Jacquie, Jan, Janet, Janice, Jaylynn, Jean
Jenny, Jordan, Josie, Joslin, Joy, Judy, Julie, Kara
Karen, Karyn, Kathy, Kim, Kristin, Kristina, LaeAnn, Lea, Leigh Ann
Leila, Linda, Lisa, Lori, Lynda, Lynn, Lula, Marian Martha, Mary
Maleigh, Meiry, Micah, Michelle, Mim, Misty Monica, Nadine, Nadja
Nancy, Nichole, Olivia, Pam, Patricia, Patty, Peggy, Randee, Rhonda
Robin, Ruth, Ruth Ann, Sadie, Sarah, Shanya, Sharon, Shelly, Sherrie
Sonya, Sybele, Sonya, Staffie, Stephanie, Susan
Tamela, Tammy, Tamra, Tara, Tasha
and always … Terry

And to my rocks:
Daniel, Dean, Derrick
and Thomas
You steady me.
Thank you

MJH

ABOUT THE AUTHOR

Mary Jane Holt comes from a really big, close, loving and supportive family. Such roots laid a strong foundation for the wealth of living experiences she has been afforded. Then eighteen years of professional nursing experience along with decades of writing, publishing and broadcasting have deepened her appreciation for the vast contrast in human experience about which she so often speaks and writes.

To reach out to her, please visit maryjaneholt.com and use the link there to send her a note.

YES, she wants to hear from you!

She also would love it if you would leave a review of this book on Amazon or anywhere else.